Japji Sahib

Published By DivineBharat

AF657921

ISBN: 978-93-344-5176-4

Publisher: Divinebharat
Email:info.divinebharat@gmail.com
www.divinebharat.co

Introduction

Japji Sahib is the most revered and foundational composition in Sikhism. It appears at the very beginning of the Sri Guru Granth Sahib Ji, the eternal Guru of the Sikhs, and is regarded as the essence of all divine wisdom contained in the sacred scripture. The word Jap means "to meditate," "to recite," or "to understand," and Sahib is a term of deep respect. Thus, Japji Sahib means "The Revered Recitation of Divine Knowledge."

This sacred composition is like a friendly guide that helps you learn about the **One Universal Creator** - the source of all truth, creativity, and wisdom that never changes. Think of it as starting an amazing spiritual journey that takes you away from fear, hatred, and confusion, and leads you toward understanding the basic principles that make everything in existence work.

Japji Sahib consists of 38 verses (called pauris) plus the opening Mool Mantar and closing Slok. Each verse contains profound wisdom about the nature of God, the universe, and how to live a meaningful life.

Japji Sahib begins with the **Mool Mantar** (the root mantra), which describes the essential nature of God. Guru Nanak Dev Ji shows us that the Creator is much bigger than anything our minds can think about or understand. Here's what this means in simple terms:

No amount of thinking can help us fully understand the Creator

No amount of meditation can capture this ultimate truth

No amount of success in the world can bring us closer to it

The only way to truly connect is by **surrendering to Divine Will** (called *Hukam*) and **living a good, righteous life**

Japji Sahib explains how life and the entire universe operate. It shows you the Creator's amazing power in four main ways:

1. **Creating** - How everything comes into being
2. **Sustaining** - How everything is kept alive and functioning
3. **Blessing** - How grace and goodness flow to all
4. **Guiding** - How every soul receives direction and purpose

Japji Sahib teaches that three key qualities help us connect with eternal Truth:

Humility - Being modest and not thinking we're better than others

Devotion - Having genuine love and respect for the Divine

Awareness - Staying alert and conscious of what's really happening around us

Japji Sahib help us discover important insights about:

- **Human limitations** - Why we can't know everything and that's okay
- **Why ego fails us** - How thinking too highly of ourselves creates problems
- **Living in harmony** - The importance of following universal laws and principles
- **Divine Command** - Understanding that everything happens according to a higher plan

This book is like a gentle but strong invitation to:

- **Meditate regularly** - Take time for quiet reflection
- **Truly see** - Look beyond surface appearances to understand deeper truths
- **Live consciously** - Make thoughtful choices based on wisdom rather than impulse
- **Recognize Divine order** - Understand that everything unfolds according to a greater plan

Through the **timeless wisdom of Guru teachings**, this book offers real, practical help for:

- **Finding inner peace** - Learning how to be calm and centered even during difficult times
- **Spiritual growth** - Developing your connection with the Divine
- **Living in tune with truth** - Aligning your

daily actions with eternal principles
- **Flowing with life's natural rhythm** - Moving with grace through life's ups and downs

This book serves two beautiful purposes:

1. **As a mirror** - It reflects back to you the infinite beauty and wonder of existence, helping you see life's true magnificence
2. **As a lamp** - It lights up the path ahead, showing you the way toward unity and connection with the One Universal Creator

The journey this book takes you on leads to one beautiful destination: **unity with the One**. This means experiencing a deep sense of connection and oneness with the Universal Creator, feeling at peace with yourself, others, and the world around you.

This book is more than just words on pages—it's a living guide that can help you discover the profound peace, wisdom, and joy that comes from recognizing and connecting with the One Universal Creator.

ik oNkaar

Sat Naam

kartaa purakh

nirbh-a-o

nirvair

akaal moorat

ajoonee saibhN

gur parsaad.

jap.

aad sach

jugaad sach.

hai bhee sach

naanak hosee bhee sach.

Pauri 1

sochai soch naa hov-a-ee
jay sochee lakh vaar
chupai chup naa hov-a-ee
jay laa-i rahaa liv taar
bhukhi-aa bhukh naa utree
jay bannaa puree-aa bhaar
sehas si-aanpaa lakh hoh
taa ik naa chalai naal
kiv sachi-aaraa ho-ee-ai
kiv koorhai tutai paal
hukam rajaa-ee chalnaa
naanak likhi-aa naal. 1

Pauri 2

hukmee hovan aakaar
hukam na kahi-aa jaa-ee.
hukmee hovan jee-a
hukam milai vadi-aa-ee.
hukmee utam neech
hukam likh dukh sukh paa-ee-ah.
iknaa hukmee bakhsees

ik hukmee sadaa bhavaa-ee-ah.
hukmai andar sabh ko
baahar hukam na ko-ay.
naanak hukmai jay bujhai
ta ha-umai kahai na ko-ay. 2

Pauri 3

gaavai ko taan hovai kisai taan.
gaavai ko daat jaanai neesaan.
gaavai ko gun vadi-aa-ee-aa chaar.
gaavai ko vidi-aa vikham veechaar.
gaavai ko saaj karay tan khayh.
gaavai ko jee-a lai fir dayh.
gaavai ko jaapai disai door.
gaavai ko vaykhai haadraa hadoor.
kathnaa kathee na aavai tot.
kath kath kathee kotee kot kot.
daydaa day laiday thak paahi.
jugaa jugantar khaahee khaahi.
hukmee hukam chalaa-ay raahu.
naanak vigsai vayparvaahu. 3

Pauri 4

saachaa saahib saach naa-ay
bhaakhi-aa bhaa-o apaar.
aakhahi mangahi dayhi dayhi
daat karay daataar.
fayr ke agai rakhee-ai
jit disai darbaar.
muhou ke bolan bolee-ai
jit sun Dharay pi-aar.
amrit vaylaa sach naa-o
vadi-aa-ee veechaar.
karmee aavai kaprhaa
nadree mokh du-aar.
naanak evai jaanee-ai
sabh aapay sachiaar. 4

Pauri 5

thaapi-aa na jaa-ay keetaa na ho-ay.
aapay aap niranjan so-ay.
jin sayvi-aa tin paa-i-aa maan.
naanak gaavee-ai gunee niDhaan.
gaavee-ai sunee-ai
man rakhee-ai bhaa-o.

dukh parhar sukh ghar lai jaa-ay.
gurmukh naadaN gurmukh vaydaN
gurmukh rahi-aa samaa-ee.
gur eesar gur gorakh barmaa
gur paarbatee maa-ee.
jay ha-o jaanaa aakhaa naahee
kahnaa kathan na jaa-ee.
guraa ik dayhi bujhaa-ee.
sabhnaa jee-aa kaa ik daataa
so mai visar na jaa-ee. 5

Pauri 6

tirath naavaa jay tis bhaavaa
vin bhaanay ke naa-ay karee.
jaytee sirath upaa-ee vaykhaa
vin karmaa ke milai la-ee.
mat vich ratan javaahar maanik
jay ik gur kee sikh sunee.
guraa ik dayhi bujhaa-ee.
sabhnaa jee-aa kaa ik daataa
so mai visar na jaa-ee. 6

Pauri 7

jay jug chaaray aarjaa
hor dasoonee ho-ay.
navaa khanda vich jaanee-ai
naal chalai sabh ko-ay.
changa naa-o rakhaa-ay kai
jas keerat jag lay-ay.
jay tis nadar na aavee
ta vaat na puchhai kay.
keetaa andar keet kar
dosee dos Dharay.
naanak nirgun gun karay
gunvanti-aa gun day.
tayhaa ko-ay na sujh-ee
je tis gun ko-ay karay. 7

Pauri 8

suni-ai siDh peer sur naath.
suni-ai Dharat Dhaval aakaas.
suni-ai deep lo-a paataal.
suni-ai pohi na sakai kaal.
naanak bhagtaa sadaa vigaas.

suni-ai dookh paap kaa naas. 8

Pauri 9

suni-ai eesar barmaa ind.
suni-ai mukh saalaahan mand.
suni-ai jog jugat tan bhayd.
suni-ai saasat simrit vayd.
naanak bhagtaa sadaa vigaas.
suni-ai dookh paap kaa naas. 9

Pauri 10

suni-ai sat santokh gi-aan.
suni-ai athsath kaa isnaan.
suni-ai parh parh paavahi maan.
suni-ai laagai sahj Dhi-aan.
naanak bhagtaa sadaa vigaas.
suni-ai dookh paap kaa naas. 10

Pauri 11

suni-ai saraa gunaa kay gaah.
suni-ai saykh peer paatisaah.
suni-ai anDhay paavahi raahu.

suni-ai haath hovai asgaahu.
naanak bhagtaa sadaa vigaas.
suni-ai dookh paap kaa naas. 11

Pauri 12

mannay kee gat kahee na jaa-ay.
jay ko kahai pichhai pachhutaa-ay.
kaagad kalam na likhanhaar.
mannay kaa bahi karan veechaar.
aisaa naam niranjan ho-ay.
jay ko man jaanai man ko-ay. 12

Pauri 13

mannai surat hovai man buDh.
mannai sagal bhavan kee suDh.
mannai muhi chotaa naa khaa-ay.
mannai jam kai saath na jaa-ay.
aisaa naam niranjan ho-ay.
jay ko man jaanai man ko-ay. 13

Pauri 14

mannai maarag thaak na paa-ay.
mannai pat si-o pargat jaa-ay.

mannai mag na chalai panth.
mannai Dharam saytee san-banDh.
aisaa naam niranjan ho-ay.
jay ko man jaanai man ko-ay. 14

Pauri 15

mannai paavahi mokh du-aar.
mannai parvaarai saaDhaar.
mannai tarai taaray gur sikh.
mannai naanak bhavahi na bhikh.
aisaa naam niranjan ho-ay.
jay ko man jaanai man ko-ay. 15

Pauri 16

panch parvaan panch parDhaan.
panchay paavahi dargahi maan.
panchay sohahi dar raajaan.
panchaa kaa gur ayk Dhi-aan.
jay ko kahai karai veechaar.
kartay kai karnai naahee sumaar.
Dhoul Dharam da-i-aa kaa poot.
santokh thaap rakhi-aa jin soot.
jay ko bujhai hovai sachiaar.

Dhavlai upar kaytaa bhaar.
Dhartee hor parai hor hor.
tis tay bhaar talai kavan jor
jee-a jaat rangaa kay naav.
sabhnaa likhi-aa vurhee kalaam.
ayhu laykhaa likh jaanai ko-ay.
laykhaa likhi-aa kaytaa ho-ay.
kaytaa taan su-aalihu roop.
kaytee daat jaanai koun koot.
keetaa pasaa-o ayko kavaa-o.
tis tay ho-ay lakh daree-aa-o.
kudrat kavan kahaa veechaar.
vaari-aa na jaavaa ayk vaar.
jo tuDh bhaavai saa-ee bhalee kaar.
too sadaa salaamat nirankaar.16

Pauri 17

asaNkh jap asaNkh bhaa-o.
asaNkh poojaa asaNkh tap taa-o.
asaNkh garanth mukh vayd paath.
asaNkh jog man rahahi udaas.
asaNkh bhagat gun gi-aan veechaar.
asaNkh satee asaNkh daataar.

asaNkh soor muh bhakh saar.
asaNkh mon liv laa-ay taar.
kudrat kavan kahaa veechaar.
vaari-aa na jaavaa ayk vaar.
jo tuDh bhaavai saa-ee bhalee kaar.
too sadaa salaamat nirankaar. 17

Pauri 18

asaNkh moorakh anDh ghor.
asaNkh chor haraamkhor.
asaNkh amar kar jaahi jor.
asaNkh galvadh hati-aa kamaahi.
asaNkh paapee paap kar jaahi.
asaNkh koorhi-aar koorhay firaahi.
asaNkh malaychh mal bhakh khaahi.
asaNkh nindak sir karahi bhaar.
naanak neech kahai veechaar.
vaari-aa na jaavaa ayk vaar.
jo tuDh bhaavai saa-ee bhalee kaar.
too sadaa salaamat nirankaar. 18

Pauri 19

asaNkh naav asaNkh thaav.

agamm agamm asaNkh lo-a.
asaNkh kehahi sir bhaar ho-ay.
akhree naam akhree saalaah.
akhree gi-aan geet gun gaah.
akhree likhan bolan baan.
akhraa sir sanjog vakhaan.
jin ayhi likhay tis sir naahi.
jiv furmaa-ay tiv tiv paahi.
jaytaa keetaa taytaa naa-o.
vin naavai naahee ko thaa-o.
kudrat kavan kahaa veechaar.
vaari-aa na jaavaa ayk vaar.
jo tuDh bhaavai saa-ee bhalee kaar.
too sadaa salaamat nirankaar.19

Pauri 20

bharee-ai hath pair tan dayh.
paanee Dhotai utras khayh.
moot paleetee kaparh ho-ay.
day saaboon la-ee-ai oh Dho-ay.
bharee-ai mat paapaa kai sang.
oh Dhopai naavai kai rang.
punnee paapee aakhan naahi.

kar kar karnaa likh lai jaahu.
aapay beej aapay hee khaahu.
naanak hukmee aavhu jaahu. 20

Pauri 21

tirath tap da-i-aa dat daan.
jay ko paavai til kaa maan.
suni-aa mani-aa man keetaa bhaa-o.
antargat tirath mal naa-o.
sabh gun tayray mai naahee ko-ay.
vin gun keetay bhagat na ho-ay.
su-asat aath banee barmaa-o.
sat suhaan sadaa man chaa-o.
kavan so vaylaa vakhat kavan
kavan thit kavan vaar.
kavan se rutee maahu kavan
jit ho-aa aakaar.
vayl na paa-ee-aa pandtee
je hovai laykh puraan.
vakhat na paa-i-o kaadee-aa
je likhan laykh kuraan.
thit vaar naa jogee jaanai
rut maahu naa ko-ee.

jaa kartaa sirthee ka-o saajay
aapay jaanai so-ee.
kiv kar aakhaa kiv saalaahee
ki-o varnee kiv jaanaa.
naanak aakhan sabh ko aakhai
ik doo ik si-aanaa.
vadaa saahib vadee naa-ee
keetaa jaa kaa hovai.
naanak jay ko aapou jaanai
agai ga-i-aa na sohai. 21

Pauri 22

paataalaa paataal
lakh aagaasaa aagaas.
orhak orhak bhaal thakay
vayd kahan ik vaat.
sahas athaarah kahan kataybaa
asuloo ik Dhaat.
laykhaa ho-ay ta likee-ai
laykhai ho-ay vinaas.
naanak vadaa aakhee-ai
aapay jaanai aap. 22

Pauri 23

saalaahee saalaahi
aytee surat na paa-ee-aa.
nadee-aa atai vaah
pavahi samund na jaanee-ahi.
samund saah sultaan
girhaa saytee maal Dhan.
keerhee tul na hovnee
jay tis manhu na veesrahi. 23

Pauri 24

ant na siftee kahan na ant.
ant na karnai dayn na ant.
ant na vaykhan sunan na ant.
ant na jaapai ki-aa man mant.
ant na jaapai keetaa aakaar.
ant na jaapai paaraavaar.
ant kaaran kaytay billaahi.
taa kay ant na paa-ay jaahi.
ayhu ant na jaanai ko-ay.
bahutaa kahee-ai bahutaa ho-ay.
vadaa saahib oochaa thaa-o.

oochay upar oochaa naa-o.
ayvad oochaa hovai ko-ay.
tis oochay ka-o jaanai so-ay.
jayvad aap jaanai aap aap.
naanak nadree karmee daat. 24

Pauri 25

bahutaa karam likhi-aa naa jaa-ay.
vadaa daataa til na tamaa-ay.
kaytay mangahi joDh apaar.
kayti-aa ganat nahee veechaar.
kaytay khap tutahi vaykaar.
kaytay lai lai mukar paahi.
kaytay moorakh khaahee khaahi.
kayti-aa dookh bhookh sad maar.
ayhi bhe daat tayree daataar.
band khalaasee bhaanai ho-ay.
hor aakh na sakai ko-ay.
jay ko khaa-ik aakhan paa-ay.
oh jaanai jaytee-aa muhi khaa-ay.
aapay jaanai aapay day-ay.
aakhahi se bhe kay-ee kay-ay.
jis no bakhsay sifat saalaah.

naanak paatisaahee paatisaahu. 25

Pauri 26

amul gun amul vaapaar.
amul vaapaaree-ay amul bhandaar.
amul aavahi amul lai jaahi.
amul bhaa-ay amulaa samaahi.
amul Dharam amul deebaan.
amul tul amul parvaan.
amul bakhsees amul neesaan.
amul karam amul furmaan.
amulo amul aakhi-aa na jaa-ay.
aakh aakh rahay liv laa-ay.
aakhahi vayd paath puraan.
aakhahi parhay karahi vakhi-aan.
aakhahi barmay aakhahi ind.
The aakhahi gopee tai govind.
aakhahi eesar aakhahi siDh.
aakhahi kaytay keetay buDh.
aakhahi daanav aakhahi dayv.
aakhahi sur nar mun jan sayv.
kaytay aakhahi aakhan paahi.

kaytay kahi kahi uth uth jaahi.
aytay keetay hor karayhi.
taa aakh na sakahi kay-ee kay-ay.
jayvad bhaavai tayvad ho-ay.
naanak jaanai saachaa so-ay.
jay ko aakhai boluvigaarh.
taa likee-ai sir gaavaaraa gaavaar. 26

Pauri 27

so dar kayhaa so ghar kayhaa
jit bahi sarab samaalay.
vaajay naad anayk asankhaa
kaytay vaavanhaaray.
kaytay raag paree si-o kahee-an
kaytay gaavanhaaray.
gaavahi tuhno pa-un paanee baisantar
gaavai raajaa Dharam du-aaray.
gaavahi chit gupat likh jaaneh
likh likh Dharam veechaaray.
gaavahi eesar barmaa dayvee
sohan sadaa savaaray.
gaavahi ind idaasan baithay

dayviti-aa dar naalay.
gaavahi siDh samaaDhee andar
gaavan saaDh vichaaray.
gaavan jatee satee santokhee
gaavahi veer karaaray.
gaavan pandit parhan rakheesar
jug jug vaydaa naalay.
gaavahi mohnee-aa man mohan
surgaa machh pa-i-aalay.
gaavan ratan upaa-ay tayray
athsath tirath naalay.
gaavahi joDh mahaabal sooraa
gaavahi khaanee chaaray.
gaavahi khand mandal varbhandaa
kar kar rakhay Dhaaray.
say-ee tuDhuno gaavahi jo tuDh
bhaavan ratay
tayray bhagat rasaalay.
hor kaytay gaavan say mai
chit na aavan
naanak ki-aa veechaaray.
so-ee so-ee sadaa sach saahib
saachaa saachee naa-ee.

hai bhee hosee jaa-ay na jaasee
rachnaa jin rachaa-ee.
rangee rangee bhaatee kar kar
jinsee maa-i-aa jin upaa-ee.
kar kar vaykhai keetaa aapnaa
jiv tis dee vadi-aa-ee.
jo tis bhaavai so-ee karsee
hukam na karnaa jaa-ee.
so paatisaahu saahaa paatisaahib
naanak rahan rajaa-ee. 27

Pauri 28

munda santokh saram pat jholee
Dhi-aan kee karahi bibhoot.
khinthaa kaal ku-aaree kaa-i-aa
jugat dandaa parteet.
aa-ee panthee sagal jamaatee
man jeetai jag jeet.
aadays tisai aadays.
aad aneel anaad anaahat
jug jug ayko vays. 28

Pauri 29

bhugat gi-aan da-i-aa bhandaaran
ghat ghat vaajeh naad.
aap naath naathee sabh jaa kee
riDh siDh avraa saad.
sanjog vijog du-ay kaar chalaaveh
laykhay aavahi bhaag.
aadays tisai aadays.
aad aneel anaad anaahat
jug jug ayko vays. 29

Pauri 30

aykaa maa-ee jugat vi-aa-ee
tin chaylay parvaan.
ik sansaaree ik bhandaaree
ik laa-ay deebaan.
jiv tis bhaavai tivai chalaavai
jiv hovai furmaan.
oh vaykhai onaa nadar na aavai
bahutaa ayhu vidaan.

aadays tisai aadays.
aad aneel anaad anaahat
jug jug ayko vays. 30

Pauri 31

aasan lo-ay lo-ay bhandaar.
jo kichh paa-i-aa so aykaa vaar.
kar kar vaykhai sirjanhaar.
naanak sachay kee saachee kaar.
aadays tisai aadays.
aad aneel anaad anaahat
jug jug ayko vays. 31

Pauri 32

ik doo jeebhou lakh hohi
lakh hoveh lakh vees.
lakh lakh gayrhaa aakhee-ahi
ayk naam jagdees.
ayt raahi pat pavrhee-aa
charhee-ai ho-ay ikees.
sun galaa aakaas kee
keetaa aa-ee rees.
naanak nadree paa-ee-ai

koorhee koorhai thees. 32

Pauri 33

aakhan jor chupai nah jor.
jor na mangan dayn na jor.
jor na jeevan maran nah jor.
jor na raaj maal man sor.
jor na surtee gi-aan veechaar.
jor na jugtee chhutai sansaar.
jis hath jor kar vaykhai so-ay.
naanak utam neech na ko-ay. 33

Pauri 34

raatee rutee thitee vaar.
pavan paanee agnee paataal.
tis vich Dhartee thaap
rakhee Dharam saal.
tis vich jee-a jugat kay rang.
tin kay naam anayk anant.
karmee karmee ho-ay veechaar.
sachaa aap sachaa darbaar.
tithai sohan panch parvaan.
nadree karam pavai neesaan.

kach pakaa-ee othai paa-ay.
naanak ga-i-aa jaapai jaa-ay. 34

Pauri 35

Dharam khand kaa ayho Dharam.
gi-aan khand kaa aakhhu karam.
kaytay pavan paanee vaisantar
kaytay kaan mahays.
kaytay barmay ghaarhat gharhee-ahi
roop rang kay vays.
kaytee-aa karam
bhoomee mayr kaytay
kaytay Dhoo updays.
kaytay ind chand soor kaytay
kaytay mandal days.
kaytay siDh buDh naath kaytay
kaytay dayvee vays.
kaytay dayv daanav mun kaytay
kaytay ratan samund.
kaytee-aa khaanee kaytee-aa banee
kaytay paat narind.
kaytee-aa surtee sayvak kaytay

naanak ant na ant. 35

Pauri 36

gi-aan khand meh gi-aan parchand.
tithai naad binod kod anand.
saram khand kee banee roop.
tithai ghaarhat gharhee-ai
bahut anoop.
taa kee-aa galaa
kathee-aa naa jaahi.
jay ko kahai pichhai pachhutaa-ay.
tithai gharhee-ai surat
mat man buDh.
tithai gharhee-ai suraa
siDhaa kee suDh. 36

Pauri 37

karam khand kee banee jor.
tithai hor na ko-ee hor.
tithai joDh mahaabal soor.
tin meh raam rahi-aa bharpoor.
tithai seeto seetaa mahimaa maahi.

taa kay roop na kathnay jaahi.
naa ohi mareh na thaagay jaahi.
jin kai raam vasai man maahi.
tithai bhagat vaseh kay lo-a.
karahi anand sachaa man so-ay.
sach khand vasai nirankaar.
kar kar vaykhai nadar nihaal.
tithai khand mandal varbhand.
jay ko kathai ta ant na ant.
tithai lo-a lo-a aakaar.
jiv jiv hukam tivai tiv kaar.
vaykhai vigsai kar veechaar.
naanak kathnaa karrhaa saar. 37

Pauri 38

jat paahaaraa Dheeraj suni-aar.
ahran mat vayd hathee-aar.
bha-o khalaa agan tap taa-o.
bhaaNdaa bhaa-o amrit tit dhaal.
gharhee-ai sabad sachee taksaal.
jin ka-o nadar karam tin kaar.
naanak nadree nadar nihaal. 38

Salok

**pavan guroo paanee pitaa
maataa Dharat mahat.
divas raat du-ay daa-ee daa-i-aa
khaylai sagal jagat.
chang-aa-ee-aa buri-aa-ee-aa
vaachai Dharam hadoor.
karmee aapo aapnee
kay nayrhai kay door.
jinee naam Dhi-aa-i-aa
ga-ay maskat ghaal.
naanak tay mukh ujlay
kaytee chhutee naal. ||1||**

9 789334 451764

Printed at Repro India Ltd.